Take any train

a book of gay men's poetry

edited by Peter Daniels

The Oscars Press

The Oscars Press, BM Oscars, London WC1N 3XX

ISBN 1 872668 00 3

Cover photograph by Mary Jo Bang

Cover design by Pictures Pens Lens, 42 Pitman House, Tanners Hill, London SE8 4PT

Typesetting by Counter Productions, PO Box 556, London SE5 0RL

Printed and bound by Billing & Sons, Worcester

The Oscars Press is a member of the Association of Little Presses, and the Small Press Group.

CONTENTS

ACKNOWLEDGEMENTS

Previous appearances of poems as follows:

"Give Me Back My Man" in America in *RFD*; and with "Clean Slates", in *Salt and Honey* (GMP, 1989).
"Be Prepared", in an earlier version, in *A Queer Tribe*. "The Dark Piano" in *Orbis*. "German Lesson" in *Foolscap* and the runners-up anthology for the Poetry Business 1989 Pamphlet Competition.
"appealing to me" in *The Performing Oscars 1987*.
"Frank's Song" as part of the 1988 Swarthmore Lecture *A Minority of One*, published by Quaker Home Service.
"Dancing Kid" in *Not Another Threesome* (Oscars Press, 1990).
"Summer Solstice" and "Picture Postcards and an Object" in *Rope Boy to the Rescue* (North and South), and *Crossing the Frozen River* (Paladin).
"Il Traviato" in *Gairfish*. "Persuasion" in *Poetry Review*.
"For a Dead Friend" and "Hey Dad" in *Cottage Cream* (Oscars Press).
"Diana Dors at Harpoon Louie's" in *Towards Gay Zion: poems 1970-1985 by Adrian Flick*.
"Yourself alone" in an anthology by Frogmore.
"at the/Springvale/homestead" in *Foreign Parts* (de Blackland Press).
"White Knights" in an earlier version in *Cottage Cream* (Oscars Press).

Many thanks to Carl Morse, without whom nothing would ever happen, to Gilles Cremonesi for valuable advice and encouragement, and to my colleagues for putting up with me.

Financially assisted by Greater London Arts

INTRODUCTION

This book is not definitive or comprehensive: it is a selection of poems, chosen because I find in them what Marianne Moore called "a place for the genuine" (in "Poetry"). And they are gay men's poems. What is the point of this?

The motives behind most anthologies should probably be looked at more often than they are, but they exist because it is found useful to gather particular kinds of verse in books. Poems have this in common with recipes. So what *is* "gay poetry"?

There are questions here of voice and audience, as they meet in the poem. Whether the emphasis is on an author's statement or a reader's assumptions, we have to negotiate the shared experience, the common ground that goes with these texts. At least in "a book of gay men's poetry" we start from a certain position, and then we can be as tactful or uncompromising as the need arises.

Much of the time it may be of no special use to be called "a gay poet" and many poems will speak to any audience: I agree with Neil Powell (*PN Review* 58, 1987) that this is not tied to the obvious subjects: "there are poems about landscape — Auden's 'In Praise of Limestone', say, or Gunn's 'Flying Above California' — which display a gay sensibility". But does this "sensibility" get through to people who aren't part of it? Even clearly gay material can baffle heterosexual readers, as I have witnessed in workshops. An instance in this book is Steve Anthony's "Diskobolos", where "caught / between envy / and desire" captures for me an essential homoerotic combination of wishing-to-be and wishing-to-have. I don't consider it a failure of the poem that some heterosexuals found this hard to grasp.

Most of these poems are directly about being a gay man, sexually, emotionally, politically. There is less outright polemic than I first expected: but whatever else happened to the ideas of Gay Liberation, the eighties certainly confirmed that the personal is political.

One reason for this has been AIDS. This is getting no easier, as an experience, or as a subject for poetry. It is so huge and so close, we can usually only focus on part of it at a time, and various agendas easily clash — political, scientific, ethical, educational. The personal-as-political does not often enable one individual to cope with all the issues at once, *and* handle the private struggles. Often we write about AIDS through personal elegies, and several are included here. The commonplaces of love and death are still to be written about though every poet from the beginning has done them already, because every human being shares in them; while AIDS brings its own elements into the picture, as the First World War, the Holocaust, and other disasters have done at other times in other ways.

During the eighties, specifically gay men's writing and publishing developed its presence, but without the dynamism of the lesbians, especially in poetry. Lesbian cultural confidence seems to me of a piece with their political energy, especially in the Clause 28 campaign (the famous abseiling into Parliament), and lesbian poetry benefits from the strengths of women's publishing, including a keen and demanding readership. It suggests that we need to consider gay men's poetry as part of something else, ubiquitous but unlooked-for. What *is* "men's poetry"? What do men want, and why do they write about it?

Peter Daniels

STEVE ANTHONY

Diskobolos

Two young men, naked
   to the waist,
         are spinning
a frisbee between them,
   their bodies
         perfecting
the changing arc.
   Facing me, one
         is bronzed
and muscular, his torso
   firm as Myron's
         athlete,
as he draws his arm
   back for the
         fling
or stretches to catch
   the disc.
         The sun
shines on their game,
   they are
         summer.
I am caught
   between envy
         and desire.

Our Share of Light

for Bob

Lighting a ten-franc candle,
I set it among the others
glowing in the cathedral.

I watch it add its share
of light and shadow
to the rows of petitioners here.

This one isn't a prayer
for Jesus or anyone else
but ourselves to answer.

It's just a small flame
for two refugees
from the night rain

of a half-known city, two friends
talking and drinking
into the night. But when,

all too soon, it goes out —
somehow it will stay
alight, our own pilot.

STEPHEN BOSWELL

Love in a Cold Climate

if I didn't say
much if I said
too much that meant
too little
it's because I've never known
my heart till now
it's a foreign country
the man in the grocer's
said "BY GINGER it's cold"
I wanted to throw his
cucumber in the air
BY GINGER
my heart has been leaping like
a salmon
and BY GINGER

it's been cold

Train of Thought

no heat on the train
just a can of cold air
and a November night
but if you should look out
past the garden swing
and the washing
to the railway line
as you make cocoa
or fill a hot water bottle
you'd think us snug in
our compartment
if you could see our gold reflections
going home across the numb land
but we are not asleep
and if we stare at the darkness
it is only for a better glimpse
of each other in the glass
I store my thoughts
behind my upturned collar
and in my corner
design a communication cord
for the two of us

PETER BRADLEY

On a Snapshot of Cavafy's House

The door was half open, as always,
To the undistinguished house of the poet.
(And while he tries to write this poem in the Underground,
A young man stands by him, dark-haired, serious,
A face of marble, stubbled, and rouged from his shave;
The young man does not look at him once.)
The street wall has lost some of its plaster,
You can see the bricks underneath
And the lintel too has bits chipped off
By going and coming of wooden furniture.
(He looks at the empty seat where a handsome man had sat.)
There is no pane in the fanlight,
Just a grille of iron finely bent into curlicues
Which kiss the shoulder of the boy on his way to see the poet
After the half-open door, through the well-scuffed hall
Up to that quiet room where the poet writes
And, sometimes, kisses the bare shoulders of boys.
The shutter opens. (The poem begins).

Two Poems of Remembering

Colm Clifford/O'Clubhan (1955-1989)

I want a poem
Tall, angular
Like you
No nastinesses
Ironed out
Quarry in that
Ore-rich earth
For iron you
Burn away the shit
In the fiery furnace
— Oh too hot for mortals —
Till your liquid
Runs lively lucid
Scorching to touch,
Can't find no mould, Colm, to catch you.
Your cold metal tears into loam
Proud and raging
Hurtful and hurt.

Jim Ennis (1956-1989)

With secret gestures of the artist
He arranges dangers and prosaics till,
One graceful sweep to the mouth — lit taper in hand — and
Whooooshhh! and
Whooooshhh!
— Wendy Wattage is breathing fire.
Tottering on stilts through Oval car park,
'e spreads his most elaborate dress,
Light organzie and slim bamboo,
Until he straddles worlds fantastically.
But in the pain and glory of blazing out
'e always kept a tapestried room
Visited by him alone.

ALAN BRAYNE

Our Shadows

Our shadows met today in the park,
The selves we hide away in the dark;
You were the emptiness I sought,
The escape from thought.

Your wedding ring glistened in the sun,
Your patchwork life unravelled, undone;
You needed a man's touch
On your skin's keen blush.

Through the undergrowth, rustling the dry green,
Soak our flesh in sweat to wash it clean;
But the touch we yearned for most
Was fleshless, a ghost.

There was truth & trust wrapped in the swift embrace
Of strangers who could vanish without trace;
Their light could only pass
Through clear glass.

Our shadows met today in the park,
The selves we hide away in the dark;
They slipped out from deepest shade,
Slipped out, instantly to fade.

ALFRED CELESTINE

When we make marriage,
a vague sensation like fear
lies in bed with truths.

It is clear that days
for us are nothings, and nights
cloud a modest care.

In the A to Z of cruising, lost eyes
find particular streets they think
for the night would make them happy.
Perhaps they never find the lies
hang-over the next morning in the pink.

I am so alone.
It's all wrong for me to sing.
Life is a straight line.

He no longer shares
the streetlamps, or even wants
the love left in me.

A thought at last is taking root.
It holds up the emptiness;
it grows deeper and deeper joys.
I try to forget even now the brute
with no trees on was my one happiness.

The older we get
the more certain streets become
the ones remembered.

It is hard to know
at times why this should be so
since they are speechless.

Perhaps I just refuse to see
the purpose of knowing a street
with no houses, with no futures.
Years ago I signed an option to be
a part of someone, someone with two feet.

The days since pile up.
I feel anonymous, clean
in my choice of streets.

When I make marriage
a streetlamp close by lights up:
his name is Brixton.

The Craft of Small Talk

Another argument: over water,
over streets, over trees crumbled the day
to far-off thoughts, and all that matters
had been reported, and my voice was clay.

I saw what there was to shape, and shaped it.
When it felt what my fingers were doing,
it lost in form, but to find bit by bit
what was wrong must leave my voice confusing.

Without a false note I walked the word
(a mock-up of necessary belief
in myself) down to an empty pier: heard
others like me singing and forgot grief.

The sum of wounds and wishes became joy
for days on end, and love threw me a buoy.

STEVE CRANFIELD

Two sonnets from **Tyrannick Love**

Give Me Back My Man
in memoriam Ricky Wilson

I have a secret love. My heart is burning.
But will he play the game? I know some tricks.
I'll fall into his strong arms like a fix.
I'll stir some unmet, deep, unconscious yearning
In his man's breast. Passion will mount. Tides turning.
His swelling manhood pressed. To mine. Limbs mix.
He'll see the light. (I've known since I was six.)
All parts rhyme. Yearning, burning and returning.
Surrendering the all I have to give.
I've got you under my skin. Now each day's
Dawning will bring discoveries, new ways
To mesh us. Never split. Infinitive.
Vows, hearts, exchanged. We'll die of love. Clichés,
Like viruses, need our fresh blood to live.

Clean Slates

Love, like construction, calls for many talents:
Hard graft; an eye for physical relations;
Style; tolerance of mess; a sense of balance;
A head for heights; a nose for firm foundations.
That summer was a neat repair man's act.
Your touch was felt from cellar up to eave.
You braved loose scaffolding, at last attacked
The damage nesting birds and weather leave.
Despite the fact that you denied the claim
Love can provide a long-term dwelling place,
I made you master builder all the same,
Asked for four walls round my potential space.
I couldn't trust love's craft, I needed proof.
From you I learnt how not to tile a roof.

PETER DANIELS

German Lesson

　　　　Some say, the secret
of Germans is in trees and rivers:
　　　　some reckon they
all belong to their breakfasts.
　　　　Experience their blank
cities in dull brown tiles and brass,
　　　　judge their variance and range
in cream cakes and dialect.

　　　　Daybreak in the square
is pale blue, blotchy through plane trees:
　　　　street lights are still
pushing their gold light from below.
　　　　The birds get started: I am deaf
to the nuances of their accents.
　　　　The body beside mine
I nearly comprehend by now.

　　　　Any language, it seems
in the end, generalises:
　　　　gestures, when drunk
or randy, get best understood.
　　　　Precision can only
matter, if it does, when you've got facts:
　　　　a few facts to touch,
and the less you take up, the less to carry.

Be Prepared

When I caught him in the bar I knew him when
I saw his curious ring that was his mother's:
otherwise I'd erased his face, and thought it was
yours, unluckily. Glad I'd done the wrong thing,
still I left him there with my embarrassment.
    I keep a spare torch for him in the closet:
    the batteries are obsolete now, you can't get them.

Every good boy deserves favour, and that
includes me: doing unto others, doing good
by stealth, doing the vacuuming only when alone
because it isn't done to be seen working,
wanting to be a Wise Virgin. Ready when you are:
    till then I have man-sized tissues by my lamp
    and a flip-top bin to discharge them into.

If I were a qualified body electrician
I'd connect up our moments of weakness
and demonstrate how they point, they rub.
The hand, the screwdriver, the spark - we learn
insulation, and our fantasies wear condoms.
    There's a candle for you under the bed,
    come over and hide there some time.

Rubbing together like boy scouts can start up
blazes of inflammatory behaviour, every
lifesaving effort a worse liability.
I doubt if we'd manage the heart-shaped badge,
and I don't stay up reading the instruction manual.
    For you I've put an oil can in the garage
    and labelled it "Danger".   You got a match?

No need to skin our desire, or clothe it with
tit bells to warn each other how to hurt.
Promise I won't write, if you won't read, and
I'll fix our weaknesses to glow without touching
till dawn comes up through a rubber window.
    I want a torch to hand on ahead of me.
    Go on: we shine from the sheer need of light.

The Dark Piano

In this song, there's the old piano-smell. It's a
bitter-chocolate varnish, with dust from the felt inside
lightening the hard and solid with a peppery tone.

Engineered into the steel frame is the fiction that
the strings are asleep under the frontage, while
they are all stretched, working harder than the finger
writing facts with a touch. The way some people speak.

Shut the lid: pianos happen in the dark. Once
as a child I awoke at night, positive there was an
arpeggio going on downstairs.

Was this a loud secret of my father's, putting
music about the house, as a release? For his
tune, or for the instrument? My ears or my mind?
Concentrate, practise, and play it for me.

And in this song there's a voice that draws up
a soft performance where I hear that smell.

KIERON DEVLIN

It wasn't

It wasn't the fact that you were wearing
soaked plimsolls in a muddy patch, and split
blades of grass were sticking to your turnups,
that made me grin; no, it just wasn't that.
My head had already turned with fever
at your smile; so Cheshire cat-like, giddy
with those allusions to my damp presence,
eliciting from the saturated,
rained-off past, the present tense response that
showers in summer are just what I need.

No, it wasn't that the waitress put two
sugars in my tea, when I distinctly
asked for coffee anyway, that made me
gulp it down. It was the count-to-ten,
instant adrenalin rush, seeing you
follow, when I paused, stalling, just to watch
you, detaching from your group of friends and
me, finding the grass so so interesting,
miles away from the old conversations
we had left behind, to say our hellos.

It wasn't even that our umbrellas
formed a rainbow canopy, a beam that
pierced through plum clouds and stopped me in my tracks,
which rendered clean the message: at all costs,
we must meet up, no matter when or where.
Some other lesson, barely remembered,
circle of events, careless matching, came
back in the crowd of men crushing in the
marquee, escaping the rain, drinking to
oblivion, with no trace of smile fever.

It was more a coincidence of past
doubt and present impulse that clinched it all,
counselling restraint; a hell of a bore

against well-aimed lips, targeting romance
at a loveless inner vacuum. We said,
"Hello", and the game was fast in motion.
What next? Not avoiding, not plunging on,
no safe solutions. Let's arrange a day,
and see what happens. Arousal began
already when you asked, "What's your number?"

appealing to me

appealing to me
you're still an ideal
i guess i'll
always search for,
though i'm deaf and dumb
sometimes i tie you up
in knots but its me
who's gagged and bound.

only when tongues nudge
open each vertebra,
a calyx unfolding
petals will i reach you.
the chains will drop,
perhaps, turn over leaves?
there is still some doubt.

i can't really see you grow,
moving when the earth moves
under us, you sitting
tight-assed on those jeans,

a spine dessicated by greenfly

today i sprouted foxgloves
from my fingernails

bikers pee on my ashes
the bed is continously
on fire. desire me.
and i will never sleep alone.

23

TIMOTHY GALLAGHER

6: William Interrogated in the Gents

Tell us a little about yourself.

Please.

Are you in love?

In what corner of the world did you first exercise that tongue of yours?

What corner are you straining to forget?

Who was your father?

And why on earth did your mother do it?

Was she in love?

7: William Tells

Once upon a time I had one but I lost it.

I wouldn't know.

I once had one but I lost it.

Once upon a time my mum told me to get one & I told her I would get one.

Why d'you think my mum told me to get one?

You'd think one person in the family with one was enough.

I wouldn't know.

13: A Solution for William

When the world crashes home the chances are you will feel abandoned.

It is then that this private old man chooses to turn distinct.

Isn't it a wonder that he homes in on you? Isn't the face familiar?

In the beginning he may seem a bit of a killjoy but at 3 in the morning he's a godsend.

His slow speech, his constant straining for the word, would try the patience of a saint, but then that saint isn't you.

Always remember that he's out of practice & that, in some other combination of worlds, he qualifies
                              as a lover.

But he has turned himself rare because he must protect himself &, protected, conserve the little that is known.

That the future was always this blank, that there should never have been
              so many expectations
              so many scenarios
              so many oracles.

HARVEY GILLMAN

Frank's Song

The dead have a pact with us.
Though tombs lie fallow in fields of snow
and our feet break on the dried-out clay,
they wait with us. They bear messages
on days even of great sunlight
when shadows are as short as memories.

And so you return, smiling
in a photograph, a sheepish, unassuming
inward sort of smile. Did it hover
as they drugged you to smother
your rage, your joy, your fear
of finding yourself alone
in another sort of world,
this smile that was your wall, your welcome?

All things touch, the living and the dead.
We smile, we love, we pass.
We embrace with such a force
no warmth remains except
traces of breath in the air,
sweat on the hair,
the smell of fear.

With the prints of our fingertips
we have signed upon the skin of the whole world
vast covenants of loving.
We bear each other
the messages of our flesh and of our silences.

Nothing can divide us now.

St Hilda's, Oxford

A window rattles,
somewhere a door trembles,
as if it bears within its grain
a knot of half-finished memories;
wind crosses the bridge like an army.

When I lived in this town,
limboed here between kingdoms,
there was always a half-closed door,
voices behind, secrets sported
in panelled rooms, windows hid light.

I always lived on the other side
of this monumental bridge, its arches
divided, not spanning the distances.
The evening light cast shadows
and little illumination.

Exile is borne within,
kept like a treasure in a casket,
whose lock rattles in the wind.

A casket thrown open amid bulrushes
yet bears a child whose face is light.

DINYAR GODREJ

Deaths of the Concubine

How nice to be your concubine
fifteenth fiddle to a cracked bass
squeaking, Wuv you.
In November it's gay Paree
land of flashbulbs
sexy kids.
Creep
throw a stone at your own heart
and it will stick.
Tentacular eyeballs
slimy antennae,
you hunt down
lust's steep canyon.
Drop.

☆

The dream cracks open
maggots within its shell.

The house settles, inevitable,
a serrated snare.

A cat approaches his bowl and will not eat:
he stalks the short corridor.

And I remember fever, promises, "forever"...
It all clangs shut. A compact, irredeemable.

Years of love-convulsion must be dumped.
Ego's scrapyard is the new territory.

It's difficult.

☆

Three vodkatonics in high spirits
entertainment for the takers.
Watching the lover dissolve into nothing
tart on satin, an endless bed.

Concubines mustn't fall in love
only learn the trade —
the right shade of skin,
a smile at a decisive moment
and the subtle art
of disappearance.

A Confession

Mum cried, Dad
shut up.

I floated out
of the moment.
A red plastic tablecloth
spawned outward in my vision.
Flushed in the wake
of what I'd said
we sat
tentatively intimate —
three separate wells in which
distinct ropes uncoil
buckets plummeting
to silvered darkness.

A distant splash.
This wringing of hands.

We Persist

for Bart

Because you make me want to discover
you by still waters
in the clearing, alone, unadorned
and feel Africa in your spine
centuries meshing in your voice
and believe.

Because sometimes the focus narrows
to stale looks in smoky bars
fetor in the rumpled bed
equating j.o.'s with angst
and pockets emptied by alcohol
with poverty.

Because you know when your tongue
rolls around mine it's really
the hand of a drowning kid
and our fierce warmth, perhaps
consumption, a flood of symptoms
seeking no cure.

And in the dark, on the streets, behind walls
I hear them cry, *Give it up, give it up*
And fists clench, teeth emerge
eyes bore you through from nowhere —
but we persist, creating no myth
shaping no reasons or explanations
just because.

D. I. HARRISON

Provocation

don't look at me
with such
provocative eyes

I'll use you
if you let me in
I'll break you

a stitch in time
will sew you up

I've lost a fortune
and you're just

a small coin
I'd throw
at a beggar

don't look at me
with such
provocative eyes

I'll spit you out
from the other
side of us

cain & abel

People's talk boring in my brain
Over nothing at all
The petty squabbles —
                        slowly killing me like Cain
A stupid mess in the hall
Who cares? Not me. No way.
But nobody gives a damn what I say.

Behaving like children?
Yeah, fine for the kids!
But when two so-called men
Both off their lids
Pick an argument
Over ownership
                of a kettle of water
I'll just go for a walk
                  sit on a bench
leave them at the slaughter
I've got to get OUT — I'm driving down
                              their lane
And they're slowly killing me
                like Cain

Goes on all day long
My head is exploding
No other song
— ding, ding, ding
Musical chairs with only one seat
The losers? They can't escape
They may win tomorrow, meanwhile they bleat
"Liar", "Thief". It comes on a tape.
Bathwater slurping away down the drain
No plug and it's slowly
                killing me like
                    Cain

I'm jaywalking down through the middle of the road
Everyday hit
Because traffic both sides
                    has no highway code
Slow it a bit
I'll do my best. What I can.
I'll be friendly to all
But I'm no special man
And let me alone in the hall
'Cos treating me like I were my label
Is the reason behind why I'm slowly
                              dying like
                                    A
                                  bel.

Dancing Kid

the dancing kid has split
with his man, the dancing
kid came round that night
when his ego needed someone
to believe him kissable show
tenderness with a hand held
and a leg being stroked

no lying being discoed round
me, if the dancing kid's man
gave a call the dancing
kid would disco dance back
whilst I would be partnering

space; this is understood it's
                    the way
                    of love

LEE HARWOOD

Summer Solstice

Farm boys tramp home aching from the fields.
They know where they're going, though don't
as they plod past the decaying mansion
overhung with dark trees and surrounded by damp undergrowth.
Two more miles to go and then the familiar lit rooms,
the drawers of known possessions, the familiar smells.
They will wash, eat and go about their evening business.
But it's all far from being that simple and innocent.
Small heaps of possessions litter the landscape.
Funerals are strategically placed throughout the years.
Even rushes of vague but powerful emotions, dumb love
and feelings that cut mazes in the heart.
They pass the darkening hedges and copses
too tired from their labours to care or notice whatever,
though the next morning it could be changed possibly.
In the spacious rooms of the mansion the wind sighs
under the doors along the staircases
from the stone flagged kitchen to the cramped attics.
"Long ago and far away" a story could begin
but leaves the listeners somehow dissatisfied,
nervous on the edge of their chairs leaning forward
in contorted positions.
                              Waking up one day
they could set off in another direction, fresh and foreign.
They could but seldom do, so cluttered are they
and rightly distrustful of such snap solutions.
                    The farm boys proceed
to the fields, again, or turn to the factory towns.
There are glimpses caught in the dusky woods
or on a fresh summer dawn of unknown skies,
unforgettable and dazzling in their beauty. But then
the long day stretches ahead. The stirred dreams settle down
with the dust, beyond grasp or understanding.
The unseen night birds calling calling

34

Picture Postcards and an Object

for John Giorno

The grey ochre building seen vaguely
in sunlight. Trees in foreground.
Mediterranean even. Calm warm surface
with the tremble of nerves, hysteria, beneath.

To rush into the palm filled lounge to
wicker chairs and tables, and cool tiles underfoot
— hotels with strutting peacocks screeching in the grounds —
and then stop, twisting and turning, and out.

No, the calmly worried look of the madonna
in a cracked fresco doesn't help. She's
more resigned than knowing. You know?
Can strit-strut whichever whichaway but "no likee".

The sages can plod up their ivory mountain
— a few tricky bits where a piton wouldn't go amiss —
to another day on the heights.
But another day on the heights.

Late night who cares. You know?
The buildings obscure in the darkness and
the music folds out. I kiss your sweating cheek.
No servants to summon. No bells to ring.

I like your black boots, but this isn't a love song.
Your shirt soaked in sweat as you "lay it down",
tell "them" "how it is", or poke their assumption.
Poke what matters, dear man, if then.

But all these blocks of stuff get moved around
and we swagger out into the night
fired with the thoughts and the heat of it all.
And the anger and mirrors feed each other somehow,
feel clear for a moment.

KENNETH KING

Forever Antrim

Having travelled extensively it finds itself
here, where now is the agony of the moment.
Ingredients of desire rage & disgust
simmer in a stew to be eaten greedily,
providing stamina for the town to commute
to the countryside from whence it came,
cream-grey sheep on green forever.
God's will, bright & beautiful, is hammered
to every ninth tree trunk, fighting the good fight.

Its problem is my problem:
I seek a way out but I don't know
where I'm going let alone who's going
with me. Does anyone
in this massively gentle dusk?

In which again I find you as you
were, small & puzzled by the landscape
which deceives with its looks of kindliness.
You, eight years old, with dark mussed
hair & swinging satchel, shuffling down
a lane to kingdom come.
You sir, they snap, don't belong,
never will, & are thereby dispossessed.
The tension of that memory is you.

The Oysters

Listen to us. Breathing chords into sound
shaped by tongue teeth & lips —
the end product corked bottles containing notes
which drift off into a sea of ... talk.
Rolling in the shallow troughs of waves, pulled by
wandering currents, the monologues continue:

That hot pants aunt of mine in Clacton is
flying out again to her toyboy Greek in Crete. &.
The cat, whilst deprecating the desecration &
profanation of our civilisation,
still sat on the mat. Or.
Given this alienation our greatest need
is for contact, as the moon

on any body of water large or small.
There exists a meter sensitive enough
to register the lunar tides of a cup of tea.
It's true. Required to open for food at the
exact instant of high tide when
the moon is over their bed, the oysters

obey, eagerly. To prevent dehydrating
they must close at ebb tide.
A thousand miles from home imprisoned in a
laboratory tank doesn't fool them at all.
They still obey the moon, opening & shutting with
the time of their original location. At one point

I gathered that you'd soon move overseas —
the question of remaining in touch a mauve
shell fractured in the shingle between us.

EDWARD LUCIE-SMITH

A Former Lover

It's ten years since I heard, and
then, one day, a letter comes.
It's neutral stuff, until I
delve into the envelope
again and find your photo,
handsome still, and not a line
to tell me why you sent it.
A week, a fortnight passes.
Now, one night, the phone, with "Guess
who this is?" I do at once,
and sense the link that joins our
lives, as they were joined before,
and see you naked, open
to my touch. What did I say?
That making love with you was
like being asked to play
a violin, untutored.
It brought me its own music.
Enough. Enough. The reason
why we parted has not changed.
We liked each other's bodies —
flesh more attuned than spirit.
Indeed, we are closer now,
remembering might-have-beens,
planning to meet, and knowing,
as we say it, it won't be.

Undressing

Stripping off, peeling, shucking —
getting ready to offer
(with so many half-muttered
shame-faced excuses) yourself.
How could I refuse you now?
The heat in the room is not
merely the fire or the drink.
It rises up from my heart.
I love you for making this gift,
though now it is mine I am
no longer perfectly sure
that I truthfully want it.
And yet how touching they are,
these small unknown details
which enter the stage one by
one. A mole, A gold chain. A
nipple. A scar. I number
them gratefully now, the small
tokens — now it is over.

EDWIN MORGAN

Il Traviato

That's my eyes at their brightest and biggest.
It's belladonna. I've a friend who. Not that
I'd ever use too much, did once, came out of
delirium after a week of sweats, you learn. But
I'm so pale now, some men like the contrast
as I stand in the park with my eyes burning,
or glide among the poplars, they're thin as I am
but seem to manage, get their light, get nourished
as I get trade although the Wraith's my nickname.
I ought to be in bed, probably, maybe.
In any case, my lover sends me out now,
he says it's all I'm good for, bring some money.
He hides my razor till I'm "interesting",
a chalky portrait ruffed in my black stubble.
I mustn't be too hard on him. The years we.
It all comes down to what kind of constant
you believe in, doesn't it, not mathematics
but as if you had the faintest brilliance
that was only yours, not to let any sickness
douse it, or despair creeping with a snuffer.
I sometimes think I wish it could be ended
— those hard-faced brutes that hit you at the climax —
but then I go on, don't I, as everyone
should, pressing through the streets with glances
for all and everything, not to miss crumbs of
life, drops of the crowded flowing wonder.

Persuasion

You never thought much of the darkness, did you?
You wanted everything so open, open —
I said it could not be — you laughed, and shook me,
and pointed me and swivelled me to windows,
doors, rivers, skies — said it must be, must issue
right out if it was to have any honour —
what: love? — yes: love; it must seal up its burrow,
must take a stair or two, a flight or two, for
poles, horizons, convoys, elevations —
but tender still to backcourts and dim woodlands.
Oh, never ask where darkness is if light can
break down the very splinters of the jambs — be
sure I know you can take in the sunlight
through every pore and nothing will be blinded
or shrivelled up like moth in flame or crippled
by some excess of nakedness — just give it,
your intelligence, your faith I really mean, your
faith, that's it, to see the streets so brilliant
after gales you really can go out there,
you really can have something of that gladness,
many things under the sun, and not disheartened,
so many in their ways going beside you.

MARCELLUS j. MUTHIEN

The Creation

I have first seen you
in a magazine
my eyes rolling like pearls of sweat
down the dark contours
of your body — taut as a bow

I have searched for you
everywhere
but when I got there
you were gone

have you ever been there

where I could look
I have
but

have you ever been

dreamed up
tonight I will
blow you to life
and my fingers will frantically feel
the ebony wood sculpture
muscle to life

and will it be true
I would need to know

have you ever

like wood burnt black and polished to perfection
glowed with a light of your own
I will ignite you
and let your dark nipples nestle
in the round softness of my lips

and you will come into me
with your halo of pubic hair
to make music like magic
from rhythm into rhyme

have you

lavaed into me
then come watch
my beautiful brown body
move glisteningly in the mirror
before the morning sun
would make me search for you
I will have you know
that I have made me
for you and you for me to come

have

Johannesburg, South Africa

of love of g

Tonight
when sitting in the company of a book
with no one reading each others eyes
and no meaningful shadows against the walls
I
am once again I am again
alone
no one
to touch no hair to brush my nose against as
often
I did with you when twining limbs in stiff plaits

I
said I wanted to be free from your clutch
remember
how freedom foamed around the bubble of our lives
and arms of winds have washed me away and
storms
of emotions have spilled bloodred on riverbanks
now
as dark shadows shade my eyes and my head has been
clawed
to reveal the man with fearsome fangs stalking
me

what
is this game of love that reduces men to worms that
gnaw
at anothers head as I am trying
here
to hang onto my sanity like a pensioner with her bag
on
a day when washing wallops in the wind of your
wisdom
because when there is no limb or love there
is
not a thing I do not feel when I'm away from
you
as I shadow into a whirl until I freeze into your life
again

Poggibonsi, Italy

44

GRAHAM PYPER

For a Dead Friend

Like a large wet
sack of sand
his body squashed itself
in its own weight
and was impossible to right

Cold
stiff
stank like blood
from a half thawed
Christmas turkey
and where my fingers
pressed it in
flesh slipped slowly back
on a half forgotten path

Inoffensive death
eyes and mouth half opened
as he died
as if to mock himself
in a mute angelic pose

He never acted better
his designer kitsch
would never dare as far
as the plastic bag
that wrapped him up

Nothing to fear
it didn't moan or groan
or leap to bite my throat
but lay and rotted
stuffed with cotton wool
against the leak

Not so much a life snuffed out
as drained away
in three long years
until it came to be
that death
was the more attractive
choice

And so I kiss him
kiss it
smooth the hair
and stay a while
make it real
and say
goodbye

Hey Dad

Hey dad
When y'threw me on the table
And y'tanned mi arse
Did I wriggle underneath yer 'ands
Like a puppy in y'fingers
Writhing head to toe
And a warm pot belly pressed against yer 'ands
And when fucking with mi mother
Though she had said no
Did she wriggle underneath yer 'ands
Like a puppy in y'fingers
Writhing head to toe
And a warm pot belly pressed against yer 'ands
Wi' mi bright red bum
And y'grinding til y'come
Tell me daddy
Which one was it
Wriggled most

ADRIAN RISDON

Diana Dors at Harpoon Louie's 19.4.84

The pub's fool compere rows
   with her accompanist.
   Diana dear, you're missed.
We wait. Impatience grows...

But here at last our High
   Priestess of Sleaze appears,
   singing how the stars
also quit the sky:

"Love being here with you...
   I face the Final Curtain..."
   Though her notes are certain,
speaks the last line or two.

"70 films: in most
   I come to a sticky end."
   Does the remark portend
a battle won or lost?

Invites enquiries from
   her audience, but cuts
   a bore's ifs and buts:
others are in the room

and this their last chance...
   Quick exit. One more wave.
   (A fortnight. Then the grave.)
That fool's back to announce:

"I *do* apologize
   for the *awful* sound..."
   Awe's somewhere around
when Diana dies.

RICHARD SCANDRETT

god

Nail hair and iron man
worm me in your cocoon

Roll me god in aching billows of your silk
Nail hair and iron man
let me writhe in your cocoon

Roll me god in billowing acres of your silk.

Nail hair and iron man
make me.

He Loves Me, He Loves Me Not

As theres no silence like our love
torn and typhooned as our past

and as theres no emptiness like our love
crippled and shorn as our embrace

and theres certainly no flower like our love
withered and colourless as our passion

i will recite you this
crushing daisies
in a daisiless field
is difficult

crushing our love
is harder still

DANIEL SUTTON

lips of indigo
and eyes so dull
reaching out
lunging in the dark
trying to grasp
another breath
another day
and all the while
the voice
just the fucking sound
of your voice
and the smell of you
sweat and bloodstains
making me crazy
i cut my hair

One Year On

You liked to keep the radio on
Because the walls were thin
And i'd open up the window
Just to let the rain come in
And wrapped up in a duvet
You'd go and make some tea
I'd sit here with a cigarette
Listening for the sea
But i only ever heard the traffic
Thundering by your door
And even when i stayed the night
You'd sleep upon the floor
The tea was bad, the sex was good
At least you taught me how
And one year on i'm wondering
What bastard's with you now

IVOR C. TREBY

Yourself alone

Sometimes you bring me wine
sometimes a kiss
one time a vial of brightly-coloured sand
i cherish these
because they show
how by degrees
your thoughts of me have grown —
Love does not practise thrift

And yet my dear
i love you just as much
or rather more
when with that kiss
but nothing in your hand
no tribute and no fare
you bring yourself alone
the full sufficient gift

at the Springvale homestead

the chance   must   be taken
for such moments   never return   we
have exchanged   words   but this is
not certain   now   two men on a wooded
hillside   beneath
a waterfall   of stars
we stand
on the precipice edge
you
        lead
                downhill
                        i
                    following
                                        stumble
fall   against your backward-reaching hand
your touch is intimate and
sure   suddenly
we are close-gripped   mouth silencing mouth
the time for question and answer   is past
our bodies need   no further permission

CHRISTOPHER WHYTE

translations from the Gaelic

In Stirling Again (Ann An Sruighlea Uair Eile)

If I didn't have this simple
talkative friend at my side
our country's knotted history
spilling in love from his lips —

each palace and battle and castle —
I'd never have dared to come back
to this tortured place so soon
after being disappointed.

The old ruins' history
distracts him, and his delight
screens me from trouble returning
the fear of your face at each corner.

On a tree-lined road, where the most
respectable bourgeois live
your house is like the chamber
of an electricity station

sending its invisible current
dangerous under each pavement
the shrill whining a continuous
threat at the limits of hearing.

Today my mind is a compass
that keeps going back to that point.
Pious builders could use me
to set their churches' rounded

apses unerringly towards
the east of their religion.
But that God is dead, his temples
are empty, his images broken.

Courage (A' Mhisneach)

More than once, as it caught
my eye with a sudden surprise
that never got less, your wrist
gave me courage to stay alive,

coming out from your sleeve
sturdy, sinewed, supple,
reminding me how a tree
rises, the powerful trunk
struggles to break free
from the earth, then loses all
rigidity in the light
foliage of hand and finger.

Your hand's quick movements were
the harvest of the tree,
each shape your fingers and palm
made in the air was a fruit
falling away from it.

I love the tree's dependence.

It's active, restless, nimble,
you can tell it has
no replica, but a partner
completing all it does;
no soliloquy this,
but a dialogue.

Hope (An Dochas)

Hope, dear heart, is nothing but
an impulse you do not control
and that you ought to unlearn.
You're like a child in front of the glittering
windows of a city store,
hungry, craving, and I'm your mother,
pulling you away, leading you back
to the dark, sad streets where our house is,
because I know we'll never be able
to buy those things, we have no chance
of ever owning or enjoying them.

THOMAS WILLIAMS

Orange

If I had a garden
I'd have an orange tree
To grow one orange a year.

The tree would grow by a window
Of my white room.
The light from the leaves would make it green.

The thorns, strong and sharp:
Nothing could get my orange
Until I chose to pick it.

The day I picked the orange,
The axis of my year:
Like Christmas only easier,
Birthdays only happier,
Beginning, middle and end
Rolled into one orange,
Pips, flesh and peel.

The pips I'd spit as far as I could,
The flesh strong with sour juice
to sting my throat,
And the peel to rip open
And make the green room smell orange

GREGORY WOODS

For Your Eyes

This is a secret.
It has never been written down before.
It was smuggled here
inside the lining of an old leather suitcase.

                               A decoy
was sent in the opposite direction
by taxi.

We closed the curtains
and sent the maid out to buy cake.
While I was making sure of the front door
you took the phone off its hook.

To maintain our anonymity we both undressed;
you were a stranger to me naked
                              as always.

By candlelight, a hand to each each corner
we unfolded the message,
profound and optimistic but
clouded by subsidiary clauses
and hedged about with conditions.

We blushed with the thrill
but afterwards in bed — when we had
torn the secret in two and each eaten
his confidential half— you confessed,
you confided
                   that you didn't understand
a word of it.
             This is it, I said
(inscrutably)
     this is the secret.

☆　　　☆　　　☆

After Sunday lunch
the breaking voices
of a solitary world

close family doors
behind them and go
kicking cans to blazes.

Their paths intersect
but they never meet.
They can hear each other

keen in the empty
streets, adam's apples
reckless with restraint.

☆　　　☆　　　☆

Injecting yourselves
throwing stones at stray cats
bumming cigarettes

caressing your zips
hooking sweaty arms
around each other's necks

spitting in the dust
sitting on doorsteps
lords of your sisters

singing filthy songs
in tomcat voices
invading my nights.

ZIGGY

Six Things To Put Me Into Shock

One.   The Cops.
I mean, stopping me twice
in one day asking me to say
things not true. Pursuing me.
Abusing me, pushing me against a wall.
Smiling. Snarling. Saying:
thank you, sir. That's all.
No sound of sorry.

Two.   A cardboard skinhead on Waterloo Bridge
who fixed me with a stare
and a snare and a Nazi kiss
on my forehead.

Three.   The Sun. Every day. And me
nude by the sea — that was o.k.
But wee queens prying into my life
asking queeny questions about
cooking, garlic and discos.
I just didn't want to know.
And us spending £1,000.

Four.   My cat,
who tried to tell me one cat thing
but because I couldn't listen,
died.

Five.   My boyfriend who kissed another man.

And six.   Dayglo yellow on an orange shirt
worn by a bright blue boy
covered in lime green dirt.

White Knights

There are no white knights
riding around on white stallions
waiting to rescue you as you sit
trapped, white from lack of sunshine,
sewing or watching afternoon movies
like a Stepford hausfrau.

The only possibility might be
a leather clad lad, tight crutched,
keys dangling, clanking like a lance,
who rides a Harley Davidson
who is restricted by his chains
who is rougher than the mainstream
but more free.
He might just be the hero.
And his armour will be soft to touch.
It's inside of him that will be hard.
That will need seeing to.

The thing is you mustn't expect him to be called
Lancealot or Hopealot or Suckalot.
If anything he'll be John or Joe.

He'll be no bad thing.
In fact he might just be good for you.
If you allow him to.

There are no white knights
              or black knights
good knights   bad knights
Sir Fistfuck or Sir Goldenshower.
No hunk will drop on you
as you ride by at some late hour;
or scale your high rise walls
and slide in through double glazing
to mount you.

You'd better get used to the idea.
Put down the tapestry. Stop waiting.

Fare Stage

The closest was using his toothbrush
and surprisingly not panicking
about catching gingivitis or tooth decay.

The nearest was watching him
in the shower then drying off
and not knowing what to do or say.

The furthest was on a No.9 crying
going off in one direction while
he waved and went the other way.

BIOGRAPHICAL NOTES

STEVE ANTHONY   was born in London in 1958 and educated at the Universities of Hull and Stirling, where he took an M.Phil. in Modern Poetry. His work has appeared in various magazines, including *Orbis* and *Encounter*, and in 1987 he received an Eric Gregory Award from the Society of Authors.

STEPHEN BOSWELL   Born Cheltenham 1947. Actor, trained Bristol Old Vic 1969-1971; played Rock Hudson's assistant in *The Mirror Crack'd*; 3 months in *Emmerdale Farm*. Poetry: *The Abandoned Labyrinth* (selection) USA 1974; *Gay News*; *Square Peg*; *The Boswell Songs* (song cycle) by Dan Locklair, USA 1987; *King Gorboduc's Fabulous Zoo*, Methuen Children's 1986.

PETER BRADLEY   "I was born in 1950 of Irish Catholic parents in Swindon, a birthplace I share with Diana Dors. After these factors, gay liberation has been a major formative influence. I support the cultural boycott of South Africa. I write plays and poems and am working on a haiku project."

ALAN BRAYNE   Born 29.6.53 in Birmingham. Founder-member of a small gay theatre group there in the mid-70s. Completed a Ph.D. thesis on the depiction of gay people in 20th century theatre. Now runs a small theatre training company, Stagecraft.

ALFRED CELESTINE   Born in 1949, and grew up in California. Began writing at university. Has been published. Now resides in London.

STEVE CRANFIELD's first collection of poems appeared in *Salt and Honey*, with Martin Humphries (GMP, 1989). He has also co-written with Annas Dixon *Drug Training, HIV and AIDS in the 1990s* (HEA, 1990), a major national study commisioned by the Health Education Authority. He lives in London.

PETER DANIELS   Born 1954, grew up in Birmingham, studied at Reading University. Has lived in London since 1982, and returned to poetry about the same time. Published *Breakfast in Bed* with Kieron Devlin and Kenneth King (Oscars Press, 1987).

KIERON DEVLIN was one-time a dresser, then a stage manager, then a waiter and is now a teacher of English, working in London. He now writes more short fiction and travel features than poetry. He took part in the Brighton Poetry Festival 1985, and his poems have appeared in *First Time* (1986) and *Breakfast in Bed* (1987).

TIMOTHY GALLAGHER was born in London in 1955. In 1981 published collection *Prosaic Poem Redeemed by Rhyme*; 1987 Oscars Press pamphlet *Carnal Ignorance*. Activities have included work for poetry venues Wooden Lambs and Cicada, and co-editing *Cobweb* magazine.

HARVEY GILLMAN was born in Manchester in 1947 and educated at North Manchester Grammar School and the Queen's College, Oxford. After several years as a teacher of French, Italian and German, he started working for the Society of Friends, where he is now Outreach Secretary. Born a Jew, discovering himself to be gay, and having become a Quaker, he is fascinated by minority culture and explored these themes in his 1988 Swarthmore Lecture *A Minority of One*.

DINYAR GODREJ Born 1965, grew up in Central India, pursued tertiary education in Bombay and is currently writing a thesis on Chaucer in the U.K. He has worked as a tutor, radio announcer, theatre and art critic, journalist, publicity officer for the Spastics Society of India, stage actor, and ghost writer. A first book of poetry is in the offing (with Praxis, Bombay). His primary impulse, as far as poetry is concerned, is to tell it as it sometimes is. Major passions are honesty, variety, and an absolute sweetie called Bart.

D. I. HARRISON David Ian Harrison was born 1958 in Sussex. Went to Portsmouth Polytechnic, graduated in 1983. Since then working in the field of mental health. Published in *Not Another Threesome* (Oscars Press, 1990).

LEE HARWOOD Born 1939, since 1967 has lived in Brighton. Has had many books of poetry and translations published since 1965, and included in numerous anthologies. His most recent books are *Rope Boy to the Rescue* (North and South) and *Crossing the Frozen River* (Paladin), both 1988.

KENNETH KING Born and educated in Sydney, Australia, he has spent his entire adult life in the UK as a professional violinist. Poems have appeared in *Counterpoint* and *Weyfarers*; a collection *Strange to*

Arrange published in Australia by The Saturday Centre (1982); and *Breakfast in Bed* (Oscars Press, 1987).

EDWARD LUCIE-SMITH   Born 1933. Freelance author, journalist and broadcaster, has written numerous books on art, a biography of Joan of Arc, a history of piracy and an autobiography. In poetry, has published two standard Penguin anthologies, *Elizabethan Verse* and *British Poetry since 1945*, and four collections of his own: the most recent in commercial publication was *The Well Wishers* (OUP, 1974), since when he has produced a number of portfolios and limited editions with artists.

EDWIN MORGAN   Born in Glasgow 1920. At present Visiting Professor in English Studies at the University of Strathclyde. Books of poetry include *Poems of Thirty Years, Sonnets from Scotland, Selected Poems, From the Video Box* and *Themes on a Variation*. Published a volume of translations of the gay German poet August Graf von Platen in 1978. Carcanet are now publishing his *Collected Poems*.

MARCELLUS J. MUTHIEN   Black, South African activist born 2 October 1963, from economically impoverished but otherwise enriching family and community. Battered through, but politically strengthened by, township schools and University of the Western Cape. Tried to contribute to the emergence of progressive gay groups, but as activist, took to the streets with the children, picking up people in pools of blood, while gay people searched for depth over deep cups of tea. Suffered formal state terrorism, including detention. Thwarted from further education: in quest for which, left seven-year relationship with lover, Gavin, to go to Italy on inadequate handout, facing continued racism. Currently a British Defense and Aid Fund student, doing M.Sc. in Clinical Psychology in London. Continues personal acquaintance with pain.

GRAHAM PYPER   Born 6.9.61 in Goole, Yorkshire, son of a docker and mother a housewife until she divorced and became a steelfixer in a concrete factory. Published in Cottage Cream (Oscars Press, 1988). Has worked for Outcast Theatre Company, and now with Positively Healthy.

ADRIAN RISDON   Born in 1948, educated at the King's School, Canterbury, and Gonville & Caius College, Cambridge, he has spent most of his life signing-on. Now lives in Bristol. Adopted as a baby, he recently found his natural family again. Published works include *Towards Gay Zion* (as Adrian Flick, 1985), and *Sick Man's City* (1988).

RICHARD SCANDRETT Born in Morpeth, Northumberland, in 1965, and moved to Southampton at the approximate age of 5. As soon as he could he moved to London where he studied English and Philosophy at the Polytechnic of North London.

DANIEL SUTTON "I am a nineteen year old psycho-geriatric nurse living in a hovel in Bournemouth with my hamster and a swiss-cheese plant."

IVOR C. TREBY was born in Devonport, and read Biochemistry at Oxford. He has had many poems published in the U.K., Europe, America, Australia and New Zealand; available to literary societies and private groups for talks and readings. Collections *Warm Bodies* (1988) and *Foreign Parts* (1989) from de Blackland Press; working on *In Leash to the Stranger*, the annotated selected poems of Michael Field, and *Woman with Camellias*, a third collection of his own work.

THOMAS WILLIAMS Welsh, born 1960 in Nigeria. Moved to Aberystwyth 1963, and to York 1966. Won a poetry competition aged 10, gone downhill ever since. Moved to London 1979. Three years at music college followed by assorted jobs; two daughters; now living with boyfriend in Stamford Hill.

CHRISTOPHER WHYTE Born Glasgow 1952, educated there and at Cambridge and Perugia. After eleven years in Italy returned to Scotland 1985 where he now teaches and researches Gaelic poetry. Currently preparing a bilingual anthology of the younger Gaelic poets as well as his own first collection, *Uirsgeul/Myth*.

GREGORY WOODS Teacher of English and American literature, and author of *Articulate Flesh: Male Homo-eroticism and Modern Poetry* (Yale University Press, 1987). His poem "First of May" was a prizewinner in the Skoob/Index on Censorship poetry competition 1989.

ZIGGY has Celtic roots overflowing onto his Putney balcony, and the decision of the nineties is whether to keep them dark or come out and bleach them. He has been published by GMP and the Oscars Press, and is director of How Absurd! Theatre Company, whose productions include work by Ionesco, Copi, Ferlinghetti and Brenton.